D.I.Y. MAKE IT HAPPEN

TIME CAPSULE

VIRGINIA LOH-HAGAN

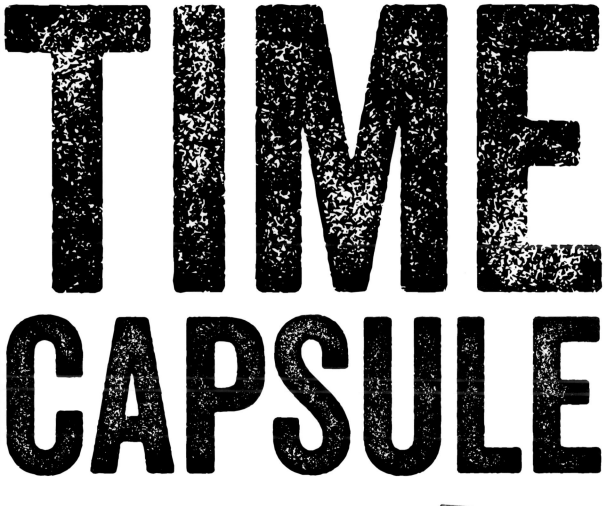

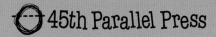
45th Parallel Press

Published in the United States of America by Cherry Lake Publishing
Ann Arbor, Michigan
www.cherrylakepublishing.com

Reading Adviser: Marla Conn MS, Ed., Literacy specialist, Read-Ability, Inc.
Book Designer: Felicia Macheske

Photo Credits: © Jeanette Dietl/Shutterstock.com,cover, 1; © Gustavo Frazao/Shutterstock.com, cover, 1, 30; © Bojan Pavlukovic / Shutterstock.com, 3; © Monkey Business Images/Shutterstock.com, 5; © Cylonphoto/Shutterstock.com, 7, 31; © Andrey_Popov/Shutterstock.com, 9; © Pixachi/Shutterstock.com, 10; © twoKim images / Shutterstock.com, 11; © Mark Herreid/Shutterstock.com, 12; © tale/Shutterstock.com/Shutterstock.com, 14; © Ramon Espelt Photography, 15; © PORTRAIT IMAGES ASIA BY NONWARIT/Shutterstock.com, 17; © Moving Moment/Shutterstock.com; Joe_Potato/iStock.com, 18; © Nicescene / Shutterstock.com, 19; © Sabphoto/Shutterstock.com, 20 © Andriy Petryna/Shutterstock.com, 21; © Christopher Futcher/iStock.com, 23; © Alexander Mak/Shutterstock.com, 25; © mezzotint/Shutterstock.com, 26; © Early Spring/Shutterstock.com, 27; © Tamara Kulikova/Shutterstock.com, 28; © Vadim Georgiev/Shutterstock.com, 29; © wavebreakmedia/Shutterstock.com, back cover;© Dora Zett/Shutterstock.com, back cover

Graphic Elements Throughout: © pashabo/Shutterstock.com; © axako/Shutterstock.com; © IreneArt/Shutterstock.com; © Katya Bogina/Shutterstock.com; © Belausava Volha/Shutterstock.com; © Nik Merkulov/Shutterstock.com; © Ya Tshey/Shutterstock.com; © kubais/Shutterstock.com; © Sasha Nazim/Shutterstock.com; © Infomages/Shutterstock.com; © Ursa Major/Shutterstock.com; © topform/Shutterstock.com; © Art'nLera/Shutterstock.com

45th Parallel Press is an imprint of Cherry Lake Publishing.

Library of Congress Cataloging-in-Publication Data

Names: Loh-Hagan, Virginia, author.
Title: Time capsule / by Virginia Loh-Hagan.
Description: Ann Arbor, Michigan : Cherry Lake Publishing, 2017. I Series: DIY projects I Includes bibliographical references and index.
Identifiers: LCCN 2016029716I ISBN 9781634721462 (hardcover) I ISBN 9781634722780 (pbk.) I ISBN 9781634722124 (pdf) I ISBN 9781634723442 (ebook)
Subjects: LCSH: Time capsules—Juvenile literature. I History—Methodology—Juvenile literature.
Classification: LCC D16 .L84 2017 I DDC 902.8/4—dc23
LC record available at https://lccn.loc.gov/2016029716

Printed in the United States of America
Corporate Graphics

ABOUT THE AUTHOR

Dr. Virginia Loh-Hagan is an author, university professor, former classroom teacher, and curriculum designer. In her time capsule, she'd include her books and black-and-white pictures of her dogs. She lives in San Diego with her very tall husband and very naughty dogs. To learn more about her, visit www.virginialoh.com.

TABLE OF CONTENTS

CHAPTER ONE

WHAT DOES IT MEAN TO CREATE A TIME CAPSULE?

Do you love recalling memories? Do you love being a part of history? Do you love collecting things? Then, creating a time **capsule** is the right project for you!

Capsules are small containers. Time capsules are collections. They hold items. These items represent a specific time and place. Time capsules are stored away. They're to be opened later.

Time changes. Time capsules capture a moment in time. They record the present.

They save it for the future. They can be big. Examples are Egyptian pyramids. They can be small. Examples are messages in a bottle.

Talk to someone else who has participated in making a time capsule. Get tips.

KNOW THE LINGO

Archaeological duty: obligation to provide future historians an accurate record of life

Archive: to store or collect historical documents or records

Cornerstone: special stone set in a building that may include time capsules

Geocapsules: time capsule containers that look like natural things such as rocks or logs

Intentional capsules: time capsules that were created on purpose and for a specific reason

Leapfrog capsules: capsules that are opened at a specific time and then resealed and set to be reopened, with people of the future adding things each time

Preserve: to save for future generations

Retrieval date: assigned date to open the time capsule

Unintentional capsules: time capsules that weren't meant to be time capsules, like shipwrecks and abandoned apartments

Vault: large underground room used for storage

Time capsules celebrate **milestones**. Milestones are special moments in people's lives. Examples are graduations and birthdays.

Some time capsules hold junk. Good time capsules have **historical** value. They tell about history. They tell how people lived. Personal items are best. Time capsules are little museums.

You'll have fun choosing your items. You'll laugh at your memories. You'll travel back in time. The best part is you'll see how much you've grown.

Communicate with future generations by creating time capsules.

CHAPTER TWO

WHAT DO YOU NEED TO CREATE A TIME CAPSULE?

Start planning. Make a list.

➡ Decide why you're creating a time capsule. This is your **purpose**.

➡ Decide who to include. You can do a time capsule by yourself. Or you can invite others. This would be a group time capsule. Several people can add items.

➡ Decide your **audience**. Audience is the people who'll open the time capsule.

Choose the type. There are different types:

➡ **Scheduled capsules have a deadline. They're meant to be opened later. They're the most popular. Choose the opening date. Consider how long you want to wait.**

➡ **Unscheduled capsules don't have deadlines. They wait to be found.**

Choose to open your time capsule in 5, 10, 25, or 50 years.

Choose the container. This is important. This holds your items. Don't let items rot.

➡ **Consider the size. Containers must be strong. They should hold the items' weight.**

➡ **Consider long-lasting containers. Containers should be sturdy. They shouldn't leak. They shouldn't rust. They shouldn't crack. Stainless steel containers are best.**

➡ **Consider containers with good seals. Containers should be airtight. They must keep out water. They must keep out light. They must keep out dust.**

➡ **Consider weatherproof containers. Containers shouldn't be affected by heat or cold. They shouldn't be affected by rain.**

➡ **Consider adding gel bags. These absorb water. Throw them into the container.**

Consider using glass jars with screw-top lids.

Decide where to store the time capsule.

➡ **Consider available places. Examples are houses or schools.**

➡ **Consider burying it outside. Keep the time capsule safe from nature.**

➡ **Consider storing it indoors. Avoid attics and basements. These areas might have leaks. Keep away from vents. Vents push out air.**

➡ **Find cool places. Avoid temperature changes. Find places that stay dry. Find places away from sunlight.**

➡ **Find places away from people. Don't let the time capsule get stolen. Avoid busy places.**

Store in locations that are clean.

TRY THIS!

Create a water bottle time capsule. Plastic water bottles last about 450 years in a landfill. This is a great way to recycle and preserve memories!

You'll need: plastic water bottle, label stickers, items that can fit inside the water bottle

Steps

1 Remove label. Wash and dry water bottle and cap. Set in sun to dry up leftover water. Make sure they're completely dry.

2 Create a label with the following information: "Time Capsule created by_____. Contents sealed on_____. To be opened on_____." Stick label onto water bottle.

3 Write a message. Include information about yourself. Roll it up. Slide into water bottle.

4 Slide in other items that represent you.

5 Bury or hide in a special place.

Collect items for the time capsule.

➡ **Match your purpose. Items should have meaning. Think about future people. What do you want them to learn about you?**

➡ **Collect personal items. Examples are photos and journals. Don't buy new things.**

➡ **Avoid items that decay. Decay is to rot. Don't include living things. Some things don't last long. Items will be trapped together. They're trapped for a long time. One bad item will affect others.**

➡ **Make sure items are interesting. Surprise people in the future. Don't be boring.**

Don't include food or plants.
They will rot.

CHAPTER THREE

HOW DO YOU SET UP A TIME CAPSULE?

For a group time capsule, send invitations.

➡ **Be clear. Tell people what to include.**

➡ **Set a date to collect items.**

Write instructions. Write as a letter. Explain things to whoever opens the time capsule.

➡ **State the purpose. Explain why you're creating a time capsule.**

➡ **State when the capsule will be opened.**

- ➡ **State who should open the time capsule.**

- ➡ **Make a copy. Include one copy with the time capsule. Keep one copy for yourself. Include a map. This is to remind you. (Some people forget about their time capsules.)**

Give people 2 to 3 weeks to collect items.

Advice from the Field
WILLIAM E. JARVIS

William E. Jarvis wrote a book about time capsules. He founded the International Time Capsule Society. This society studies time capsules. It tracks time capsules. It's located in Atlanta, Georgia. He advises, "Be anti-tech when it comes to what you put inside." Don't include technology in the time capsule. Technology will be outdated when the capsule is opened. Technology can also damage other items. Electronics corrode. They have chemicals that break down things. Jarvis advises to put in objects that show evidence of human touch. An example is a used book. Jarvis also advises to leave a location marker. He said, "People are always losing their time capsules."

Write a personal letter. Include it in the time capsule.

⇒ **Describe your life right now. Describe activities. Describe chores.**

⇒ **Describe your current interests. Describe favorite music. Describe favorite books. Describe favorite hobbies.**

⇒ **Write a prediction for the future. On opening day, see if you were correct.**

Create a label card. Do this for each item. Include the following information:

⇒ **Name of contributor. This is the person who added the item.**

⇒ **Name of item.**

⇒ **Reason for including it in time capsule.**

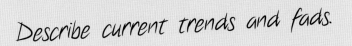

Describe current trends and fads.

Take photos of the location and send an e-mail to yourself.

Schedule the opening date. Remember the time capsule. Don't forget. Here are options:

➡ **Record the opening date in an online calendar. The opening date may be years ahead. Make a calendar reminder.**

➡ **Write down date and location. Keep in a journal. Or post on the fridge.**

➡ **Match the opening date to a special day. Examples are birthdays or holidays.**

➡ **Tell several people. Tell them the location and date. Hopefully, someone remembers.**

➡ **Host yearly parties. Do this on the anniversary of the sealing ceremony. Anniversary is the same day in a different year. Sealing means closing. A ceremony is a special event. It honors something or someone.**

CHAPTER FOUR

HOW DO YOU HOST A TIME CAPSULE SEALING CEREMONY?

Make the time capsule memorable. Host a sealing ceremony. This is a special party. It celebrates the closing of the time capsule.

➡ Invite family. Invite friends. For group time capsules, invite contributors' loved ones.

➡ Set up a table. This is for greeting guests. Provide name tags and pens. Have guests wear name tags.

➡ Consider music. Get a live band. Or make a playlist. The music should be calming. It should match the purpose.

➡ Provide drinks. Provide snacks. Keep it simple.

➡ Provide trash cans.

Give guests time to mingle.
Mingle is hanging out.

QUICK TIPS

- Don't include canned foods. Canned foods have trapped gases. They explode.

- Don't include rubber bands, paper clips, or staples. These things rust or rot. They'll ruin documents. Some magazines have staples. Remove the staples. Sew the pages together with cotton thread.

- Don't include silk, wool, or nylons. Wool and silk have a chemical that destroys metal over time. Nylons break down quickly.

- Clean any clothes and fabrics.

- Avoid including electronics. But if you do, keep wood away from electronics. Be sure to remove batteries.

- Don't polish items before sealing in time capsule.

- Don't include newsprint. Copy newspaper articles. Use acid-free paper.

- Black-and-white photos keep better than color photos.

- Use soft pencils to label items. Ink stains. Ink changes over time.

Give a **toast**. A toast is a special speech.

- Get everyone's attention.

- Give everyone a drink. Have them raise their glasses.

- Explain why you created the time capsule. State when the time capsule will be opened.

- Consider reading a poem. The poem should match the purpose.

- Thank everyone for coming.

- For group time capsules, thank contributors for adding items.

- Have everyone clink glasses. Have everyone drink at the same time.

Consider naming the time capsule. A name makes it more special. It makes it unique.

- Match the name to the purpose.

- Decorate the container.

Assign someone to take pictures of the sealing ceremony.

Remember that each item is a piece of your history that you've chosen to share.

Start packing items. Place into time capsule. Make packing a special time.

➡ **For group time capsules, call each contributor. Have contributors take turns. Allow them to share comments.**

➡ **Place heaviest items at the bottom.**

➡ **Store items in plastic bags. Store in glass jars. Wrap items in acid-free paper. This is special paper. It doesn't contain harmful acid. Acid can damage things.**

➡ **Be careful packing. Don't break anything.**

Seal the time capsule.

➡ **Make sure container is tightly closed.**

➡ **Record date of opening. Write this on container.**

➡ **Store container in special location.**

Create a **marker**. A marker is a sign. It marks the time capsule's location. These are options.

➡ Wooden sign with name and date.

➡ Natural objects like large rocks or logs. Paint a symbol on them.

When guests leave, thank them for coming.

➡ Consider giving guests a little gift. An example is a bookmark. Include the opening date on it.

➡ Remind them to come to the Time Capsule Opening Party.

Make sure container is dry and clean before sealing.

D.I.Y. EXAMPLE!

STEPS	EXAMPLES
Type	◆ Intentional and scheduled ◆ Group
Purpose	To celebrate graduation from middle school
Participants	Me and my five best friends
Where	Under a garden bench in my backyard
How long	Four years: ◆ Sealing ceremony will be on graduation day from middle school ◆ Opening ceremony will be on graduation day from high school
Container	◆ Each of us will put items in cardboard boxes with lids. We'll decorate the boxes. We'll include our names. We'll individually wrap the items in plastic bags. ◆ We'll put the boxes in a large plastic container with a tight lid.

PAST

FUTURE

STEPS	EXAMPLES
My time capsule items	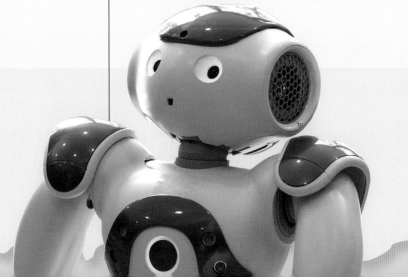 ➧ Personal letter ➧ Letter of instructions ➧ Ripped-out pages from my diary ➧ T-shirt from a concert signed by the band ➧ Favorite book with all my notes written inside ➧ Framed picture of me and my friends at an event ➧ Best essay I wrote for English class ➧ Sheet music for a piano song I just mastered, including notes from my piano teacher

GLOSSARY

acid-free (AS-id FREE) not having acid, which can damage things

anniversary (an-uh-VUR-sur-ee) a date people remember each year because of an important event that happened on that date in an earlier year

audience (AW-dee-uhns) people who observe something

capsule (KAP-suhl) small container

ceremony (SER-uh-moh-nee) a special event that honors something or someone

contributor (kuhn-TRIB-yoo-tur) person who adds something

decay (di-KAY) to rot or deteriorate

gel bags (JEL BAGZ) special little bags of chemicals that absorb moisture

historical (hih-STOR-ih-kuhl) representing history

marker (MAHRK-ur) a sign that marks something

milestones (MILE-stohnz) important moments in someone's life

purpose (PUR-puhs) reason for doing something

sealing (SEEL-ing) closing

toast (TOHST) a short speech given to celebrate someone

vents (VENTS) openings that push out air

weatherproof (WETH-ur-proof) not affected by heat, cold, or rain

INDEX

LEARN MORE

BOOKS

Caney, Steven. *Make Your Own Time Capsule*. New York: Workman Publishing, 1991.

Franco, Betsy. *Q & A a Day for Me: 3-Year Journal*. New York: Potter Style, 2012.

WEB SITES

International Time Capsule Society: http://crypt.oglethorpe.edu/international-time-capsule-society/

WikiHow—How to Create a Time Capsule: www.wikihow.com/Create-a-Time-Capsule